CONTENTS

WHAT IS A RAINFOREST?

A rainforest is a special kind of forest that grows in warm, wet places. The trees are tall, and grow closely together. There are three main types of rainforest:

Tropical forests

Tropical rainforests grow near the Equator (an imaginary line around the middle of the Earth). The climate is hot and rain falls nearly every day. The rainforest trees are evergreen trees – they have leaves all year round.

The largest area of rainforest is the Amazon rainforest, in the huge Amazon River basin in South America. There are also tropical rainforests in Central Africa, South-east Asia and Australia.

This bright yellow tree frog lives in the tropical rainforests of South America.

SAVING THE RAINFORESTS

Sally Morgan

W
FRANKLIN WATTS
LONDON • SYDNEY

First published in 1999 by
Franklin Watts
96 Leonard Street, London
EC2A 4XD

Franklin Watts Australia
14 Mars Road
Lane Cove
NSW 2066

EARTH WATCH: SAVING THE RAINFORESTS was produced
for Franklin Watts by Bender Richardson White.
Project Editor: Lionel Bender
Text Editor: Jenny Vaughan
Designer: Ben White
Picture Researchers: Cathy Stastny and Daniela Marceddu
Media Conversion and Make-up: Mike Weintroub,
        MW Graphics, and Clare Oliver
Cover Make-up: Mike Pilley, Pelican Graphics
Production Controller: Kim Richardson

For Franklin Watts:
Series Editor: Sarah Snashall
Art Director: Robert Walster
Cover Design: Jason Anscomb

A CIP catalogue record for this book is available from the British
Library.

ISBN 0-7496-3301-8 (hbk)   0-7496-3592-4 (pbk)

Dewey classification 333.73

Printed at Oriental Press, Dubai, U.A.E.

Picture Credits:

Oxford Scientific Films: cover small photo & page 4 top (Michael
Fogden), 6 top (Martyn Colbeck), 10 (Frank Schneidermeyer),
11 bottom (Nick Gordon), 12 (Edward Parker), 13 top (M.
Wendler/Okapia), 18 (Daniel J. Cox), 19 bottom (Stan Osolinski),
26 (Daniel J. Cox). **The Stock Market Photo Agency Inc.:** cover
main photo, globe & pages 1, 6-7, 8, 17, 19 top, 22-23 (J. M.
Roberts), 28. **Ecoscene:** pages 4 bottom (Andrew Brown), 9 (Simon
Grove), 14 (Alexandra Jones), 15 (Joel Creed), 27 top (Joel Creed).
Panos Pictures: pages 11 top (Arabella Cecil), 13 bottom (Ron
Giling), 16 (J. Hartley), 20 (Chris Stowers), 21 top (David Reed), 21
bottom (Jeremy Horner), 22 bottom (Fred Hoogervorst), 24 (Liba
Taylor), 25 bottom (Jean-Léo Dugast), 27 bottom (Arabella Cecil),
29 top (Fred Hoogervorst). **Environmental Images:** pages 17 top
(Mark Fallander), 25 top (Irene R. Lengui), 29 bottom (Herbert
Girardet). Science Photo Library, London: pages 23 (Peter Menzel),
Artwork: Raymond Turvey.

Cloud forests

Rainforests that cover mountains in tropical regions are called cloud forests because they are up in the clouds. The air is cooler higher up a mountain and there is more moisture in the air. Trees in cloud forests are shorter than those in tropical forests, and they are deciduous – they drop their leaves once a year.

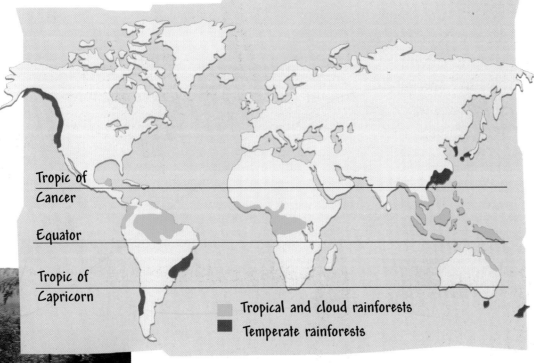

Tropic of Cancer

Equator

Tropic of Capricorn

Tropical and cloud rainforests
Temperate rainforests

Tropical rainforests and cloud forests are found around the Equator. Temperate forests are further north and south.

Tree ferns and bamboo grow in this tropical forest on the island of Saint Lucia, in the Caribbean.

Temperate forests

Temperate rainforests grow further from the Equator, where the climate is cooler. Here there are distinct seasons, when some parts of the year are cool and others warmer. Many of the trees are conifer trees, which have needle-like leaves that drop gradually all through the year. The trees are covered in mosses and lichens. There are temperate rainforests in Australia, New Zealand, North America and parts of South America.

RAINFORESTS AT RISK

In the last few years, huge fires in the rainforests of Brazil and Indonesia have hit the news. On television, we have seen dramatic pictures of the fires and the damage they have caused. Forest fires are common, so why should they worry us?

Millions of plants and animals

We should worry because forests are important. Scientists think that about ten million different species (types) of plants and animals live on Earth. The rainforests are home to nearly two-thirds of these. Some animals live among the leaves, others on tree trunks, and some on the forest floor. Because of this, scientists say rainforests have a high biodiversity (variety of living things).

In Zaire, Africa, patches of rainforest are burned to clear land for vegetable gardens. Small fires do little harm.

6

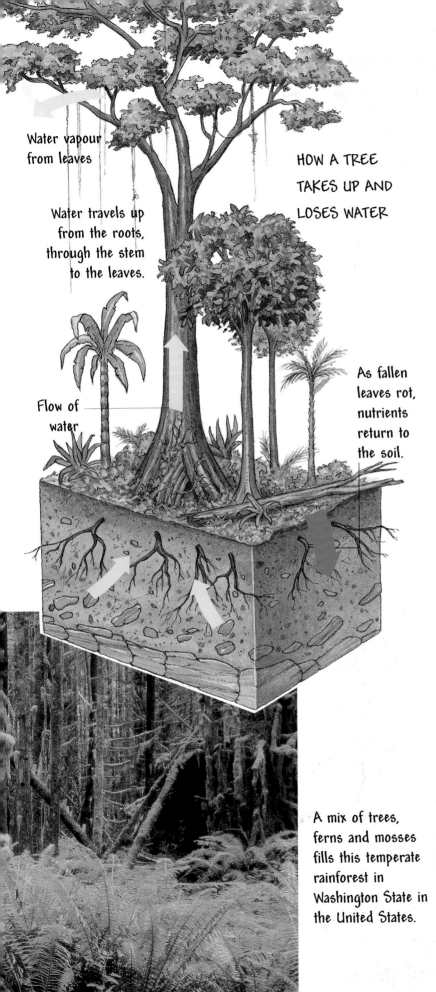

Water vapour from leaves

HOW A TREE TAKES UP AND LOSES WATER

Water travels up from the roots, through the stem to the leaves.

As fallen leaves rot, nutrients return to the soil.

Flow of water

A mix of trees, ferns and mosses fills this temperate rainforest in Washington State in the United States.

Water and climate

We should also save rainforests because they release so much water into the air that they affect the climate of the tropics. Plant roots draw up water from the ground. A lot of the water evaporates (turns to vapour, or tiny droplets) from the surface of the leaves and mixes with the air. This helps form rain clouds.

Gases in the air

Leaves use the energy of sunlight to join water and carbon dioxide gas from the air to make food. As they do this, they give off the gas oxygen.

Most living things, including trees, need oxygen to convert food material into energy for their bodies. Removing rainforests cuts down the amount of oxygen in the air, threatening the lives of many plants and animals.

Eco Thought

In a patch of rainforest just 6 kilometres square, there can be as many as 1500 species of flowering plant, 400 species of bird, 150 species of butterfly, 100 species of reptile and 60 species of amphibian.

7

IN A RAINFOREST

A rainforest is like a tall building with many floors. Each floor, or layer, is home to a different range of plants and animals.

In the canopy

The tops of the trees make up the roof of the forest, called the canopy. Most of these trees are about 40 metres tall. A few even taller trees, called emergents, poke their heads above the canopy. The canopy is full of life. Monkeys swing from branch to branch. Birds nest here and feed on the nuts and fruits.

The understorey

Beneath the canopy is the understorey. Here, climbing plants called lianas dangle down to the forest floor. Plants called epiphytes, such as orchids, cling to the trees, taking water from the air or from tree bark.

The canopy of this Australian rainforest is not particularly thick so that a good deal of sunlight reaches the forest floor.

CANOPY

UNDERSTOREY

The forest floor

Little light passes through the understorey down to the forest floor. Only small trees and palms can live in the gloom. It is damp and warm, so leaves and twigs rot quickly.

Fungi are important decomposers. They break down the leaves and release nutrients (chemicals that help other plants grow). Creatures such as termites, earthworms and spiders search the floor for food.

Eco Thought

In Costa Rica, in Central America, there is thick rainforest. A monkey could travel 65 kilometres, from the Caribbean coast to the top of the mountains, without leaving the treetops.

FOREST FLOOR

Heavy rain creates thick mud on the floor of this Indonesian rainforest.

9

RAINFOREST PEOPLE

More than 1,000 different groups of peoples live in rainforests. They have lived there for thousands of years. They get food, clothing, medicines and shelter from the forests.

In a clearing in a tropical rainforest in Papua New Guinea, men prepare fire and fruit for a feast.

Gardens in the forest

Rainforest people have learned how to farm the forests without harming them. They know the soils are thin and crops cannot grow there for more than a few years. They clear tiny patches to make gardens for crops, medicine plants and fruit trees.

After a few years they move on, leaving the old garden to become forest again. But the families return to the gardens to harvest fruits from the trees they planted.

On the Ground

In 1990, the Colombian government in South America gave back half of its land around the Amazon River to rainforest people. The government realized that they were the best guardians of the forest.

Eco Thought

The Kayapo people of the Amazon rainforest have at least one use for nine out of every ten plants which grow around the villages. Some plants are used for food, others for building materials or to provide medicines and dyes for cloth.

In many rainforests, like this one in Peru, hunting and fishing are important ways of getting food.

Uncertain future

The people of the rainforests hunt birds, pigs and deer, and catch fish. They are careful not to kill too many animals so as not to run out of food. They kill only those they need for meat or clothing.

But now, people and large companies from outside are using the forests for farmland and to provide timber. They are cutting down the trees, and the people who used to live in the forests are leaving. There is a danger that all their knowledge of the forests will be lost forever.

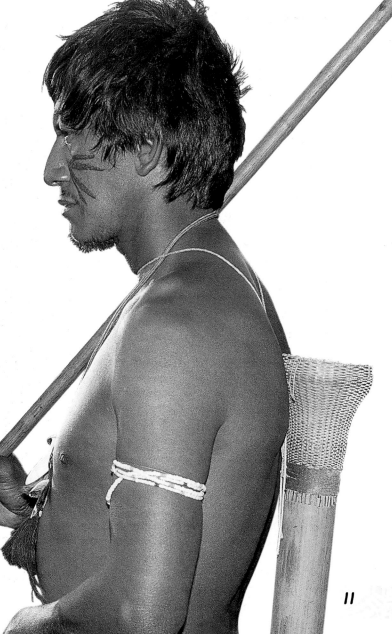

A hunter in the Amazon rainforest area of Venezuela.
He hunts with a blowpipe and poison darts, which he carries in a quiver on his back.

DISAPPEARING FORESTS

As the world's population gets larger, more food and building materials are needed. Half the world's rainforests have been destroyed to provide timber or farmland. It will take centuries for them to grow back.

This boy in Cameroon, Africa, burns a clearing in the forest. Here, his family will grow food.

Land for farming

In Central and South America, land that was once forest is now pasture for cattle. In many countries, the best farmland outside the forest is all owned by rich people. Poorer farmers need somewhere to live, so they clear forest land for farms. They grow crops, and use wood as fuel. In many parts of the world, wood is the only fuel available for cooking and for heating water.

Eco Thought

In 1950 there were just under 1,000 million hectares of rainforest in the world. Soon, this figure may fall to less than 500 million hectares. In the time you take to read this page, more than 60 hectares of rainforest will have been destroyed.

Tropical woods

Tropical wood is used a lot in building. In South-east Asia and Africa logging for timber is the main reason for clearing the forest. Timber companies build roads into the forests so they can bring in machinery to clear the forest and pull out the logs. The logs are sent by road, or floated down rivers, to ports. From the port, they are exported all over the world and used to make tables and other furniture.

In Brazil, heavy machinery that can damage the forest is being used to move trees.

Big business

Huge areas of rainforests are burned to clear land. On much of this land, cash crops (crops grown for sale) such as coffee, bananas or rubber are grown instead of fruit and vegetables for local people.

Mining, industrial development and the building of large dams all damage the rainforests, too. Even tourism is threatening some of the more popular rainforests.

These young rubber trees in West Africa will be planted in land that was once rainforest.

WASHED AWAY

In parts of the tropics (regions of the world near the Equator), there are heavy downpours of rain almost every day. About 15 centimetres of rain can fall in just a few hours. London might get that much rain in a month.

Water from the trees creates clouds and later falls as rain

A huge sponge

The rainforest is like a huge sponge. The plants soak up most of the rainwater. This evaporates from the leaves, creating mist and low cloud.

The water in the clouds falls back on to the forest as rain. The water is recycled over and over again. Some of the water drains into streams and rivers. The rainforests release this water slowly, so the rivers never run dry.

Water drains from the forest soil into rivers

A NORMAL TROPICAL RAINFOREST

A waterfall in a tropical rainforest in Australia.

Soil erosion

If the trees are cleared away, there are no roots to hold the soil. Rain washes it away. This is called soil erosion. Soil washes into streams and rivers and chokes them with mud. Aquatic (water) plants and animals that need clear and clean water die.

Without the trees, rain washes away the soil. Mud clogs up the rivers.

On the Ground

In Honduras, people are trying new ways of preventing soil erosion. They plant fast-growing plants, such as lupins, on cleared land. These protect the soil until farmers are ready to sow crops.

Less rain

With fewer trees, rainwater drains away quickly. At first, farmers have more water for their crops. But then, less water evaporates, so less falls as rain. The climate of the rainforest changes. Instead of reliable rainfall, there may be droughts.

In Brazil, rainforest trees have been removed. Heavy rains have eroded the soil and formed this deep gulley.

15

GLOBAL RESULTS

Rainforests can affect the climate in places far away from the tropics. The mass of leaves of the trees affect the amount of moisture and gases in the air. This then affects rainfall all over the world.

Spreading rain

The Sun is over the tropics all year. The heat causes water vapour to rise from the leaves of the trees, high into the atmosphere. As the vapour cools and changes back into liquid water, it creates rain clouds. The moist air moves from the tropics towards the Equator and the poles. If the rainforests are lost, less rainfall spreads out from the tropics. This could lead to droughts.

Where a rainforest is completely destroyed, the area can eventually turn into scrubland, as here in West Africa.

Taking Part

Which absorbs more heat – dark rainforest or desert? To find out, put a dark-coloured saucer of water and a light-coloured one on a sunny windowsill. Water should evaporate faster from the dark saucer because dark colours absorb more heat.

Global warming

Like most plants, rainforest trees use carbon dioxide gas in the air to make food. Carbon dioxide gas is released into the air when coal, oil, natural gas or wood are burned. Carbon dioxide in the air above the Earth traps the heat of the Sun and warms up the Earth. This is called global warming.

Burning wood

If rainforests are cleared, there are fewer trees to take up the carbon dioxide. When the trees are burned, the carbon in the wood helps form more carbon dioxide. This adds to the problems of global warming.

People in Indonesia wear masks to protect them from smoke from burning rainforests.

Eco Thought

Forty years ago, almost half of Ethiopia was covered in forest. Now there is hardly any forest and the climate has changed. There are regular droughts and, when it rains, the land floods quickly.

In Malawi, an area of rainforest has been cleared to make this tea plantation. As a result, the local climate has become drier.

RAINFOREST WILDLIFE

The plants, fungi and animals of the rainforest all have a job to do, and they depend on each other. For example, bees carry pollen between flowers. Birds spread seeds. Fungi rot the fallen leaves. If one plant or animal type disappears, others may do so too.

Mountain gorillas are threatened by both destruction of rainforests and hunting by local people.

Under threat

Many species of wildlife are only found in one small area of rainforest in the world. As the rainforest is destroyed, such animals and plants are in danger of becoming extinct (dying out).

Mountain gorillas, for example, live in the rainforests of Central Africa. The forests are being logged and this is destroying their habitat (home) and the plants that they eat. In addition, forest people kill the gorillas for food. The gorillas may be saved if the remaining forests are protected.

Eco Thought
Fifty species of rainforest animals, of which most are insects and spiders, become extinct each day.

Tigers live in rainforests in India and other parts of southern Asia. Although their habitats are now protected as nature reserves, there are now only around 5,000 tigers left in the world.

Corridors through the forest

Big meat-eaters, such as tigers, jaguars and eagles, need a large area in which to hunt. When the forests are cleared, they cannot find enough food. The animals can become trapped as though they are on an island. They are cut off from sources of food, shelter and mates.

One way to solve this problem is to create natural corridors of trees between forest areas that are protected as nature reserves.

One in three parrots risk extinction in the wild. These hyacinth macaws are in a zoo. Breeding rainforest animals in zoos is one way to save them.

RICH RESOURCES

Rainforests are rich in materials used in industry. These are called resources. Wood, such as teak and mahogany, is used in building and to make furniture. The rocks beneath the forests may contain oil and metals, such as gold, silver and zinc.

Huge numbers of logs are floated away from a tropical rainforest on a river in Borneo.

Logging

Many rainforests produce hardwood, which is tough and long-lasting. It is ideal for building and making furniture such as tables. Unfortunately, the best trees are scattered through the forest. In reaching them, loggers damage other trees and the soil, making it hard for young trees to grow.

Valuable timber

Most hardwood is sold and transported to other countries. There, it is usually sold again for hundreds of times more than the local people were paid for it. Often, this valuable wood is wasted when it is used to make throw-away objects such as packing crates and chopsticks.

Eco Thought

After logging, as many as three out of every four of the trees left behind in the forest may have been badly damaged. It takes hundreds of years for the trees to regrow fully.

This mine in Guinea in Africa is an important source of money, but it has damaged the rainforest.

In Colombia, local people extract gold from a hillside in the rainforest.

Mining

Huge areas of forest are cleared so that mining companies can reach the rock that contains oil and valuable metals. Sometimes they remove whole hillsides.

Digging quarries produces a lot of waste material and this is usually dumped on nearby land. Water running off this waste and from the quarries may be polluted and can harm the aquatic life of streams and rivers.

Taking Part

Look round your home and see if you can spot the different kinds of woods used to make furniture. Look for pine, which is called softwood, and hardwoods, such as teak, oak and beech.

NEW FINDS

Scientists believe that they have only found about one-tenth of the animals and plants in the world's rainforests. New species (kinds) are being discovered every day. Many forest plants could be the source of new medicines or foods.

New medicines

About a quarter of all modern drugs came originally from rainforests. The forest people discovered most of these long ago. They use plants to treat headaches, fevers, cuts, snake bites, toothache and skin infections.

Scientists have tested only a hundredth of the rainforest plants to see if they can be used in medicine. It is important to test more, because they may help to cure many diseases.

Eco Thought

In South-east Asia, traditional healers use about 6,500 types of tropical plant to treat illnesses. These include malaria and stomach ulcers.

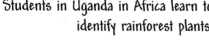

Students in Uganda in Africa learn to identify rainforest plants.

Exotic foods

Crops such as rice, coffee, bananas and peanuts all came first from rainforests. There may be around 75,000 types of edible plant in the world, but we eat only a few hundred of them. Our diets could be far more varied and healthy if we used more rainforest plants.

Making discoveries

Scientists are discovering useful rainforest plants all the time. There are fruits containing more vitamin C than oranges, and substances 300 times sweeter than sugar. One tree produces a kind of oil that can be used in diesel engines. Some plants contain insecticides (substances that kill insect pests).

No one is sure how many useful plants there may be. But if the forests disappear, we will never know.

A scientist studies a weed growing in a rainforest in Hawaii.

In the understorey of a temperate rainforest, more than 30 different types of plants are tangled together.

Taking Part

Try growing your own rainforest plants, such as an avocado or mango. Soak the stone in water and then plant it in a small pot of compost. Leave it in a warm, light place and water it regularly. After a while, a shoot will appear.

SUSTAINABLE FORESTS

Rainforests have to be conserved (protected) for the future. They must be managed in a sustainable way – some wood can be removed, but enough must be left for next year and the years after that.

On the Ground

Scientists in Peru are trying new ways of logging. They fell trees in strips just 20 to 50 metres wide. They hope that animals will cross the strips and seeds will germinate. In time, the strips become part of the forest again.

Controlled logging

One way to conserve a forest is to fell the trees in only one part of it, and leave the rest alone. Then new trees can be planted in the cleared area, or it can be left to regrow naturally.

New plantations of fast-growing teak trees are being planted in India and Central America. These trees will be felled in just 20 or 30 years. After that, the land will be replanted again.

The manager of a sustainable rainforest in Brazil carefully records the number of logs that are being taken away by truck.

Eco Thought

Rainforests at most risk from logging are in Central and South America, Central Africa, South and South-east Asia, and eastern Australia.

Replanting the forests

Deforested land can be replanted. Trees are grown from seeds in nursery gardens. When the young plants are large enough, they are planted in the forest. New forests take several hundreds of years before they have the rich variety of life found in the original rainforests. But a young forest is better than no forest at all.

Students in the Philippines are learning how to plant young trees and so help the forests regrow.

Teakwood from a sustainable forest is stored at a timber yard in Thailand.

Loggers' logo

How can you tell if wood comes from a sustainable forest? One way is to look for the logo of the Forest Stewardship Council stamped on the wood. The Council was set up in 1993. Council members check that the timber companies in rainforests are operating in an environmentally friendly way. If they are, they can use the logo.

Taking Part

If your family buys tropical timber, make sure it bears the Forest Stewardship Council 'FSC' symbol. If there is no FSC symbol, buy hardwoods that do not come from tropical forests, such as oak, beech or sycamore.

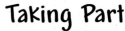

CARE OF THE FORESTS

Deforestation is going on all the time. It is important that action is taken quickly to save the remaining forests.

Protected parks

One way to make sure that a rainforest is conserved is to make it a nature reserve or national park. Most countries have set up national parks, where the forest is protected from logging and farming.

Ecotourists

Tourists can help by bringing in money for local people. 'Ecotourism' is tourism based on ecology, which is the study of the relationships between living things and their surroundings.

Visitors are taught about and helped to understand the places they visit. They stay in the rainforests in small hotels made from local materials, and they use renewable energy, such as solar power. The number of tourists is controlled so the environment is not harmed.

Eco Thought

Ecotourism is booming in Central America. About ten per cent of the land in Central America is either a national park or a nature reserve. At least five new parks are set up each year.

In this rainforest in Malaysia, young orang-utans are being cared for by a forest ranger. Locals can find jobs that protect rather than destroy the habitat.

Involving the people

Cutting down trees and selling timber is a quick way of making money. But rainforest people now realize that if they look after the trees, they will be able to earn money for many years.

It is important for them to find ways to earn money without harming the rainforest. They can collect and trade rainforest products, such as nuts for eating and for making oils. If the rainforests are conserved, people and wildlife can both benefit.

Rainforest ecotourists take a river journey in Iguacu National Park, Brazil.

Forest people can earn money from traditional crafts, like these potters in Peru.

WHAT CAN WE DO?

The future of the rainforests is important to everyone.
People and governments need to work together to
make sure this precious resource is used well.

The Earth Summit

In 1992, there was a meeting in
Brazil called the Earth Summit.
Politicians and experts from 150
countries discussed biodiversity,
the importance of rainforests
and global warming. They drew
up a biodiversity action plan –
they agreed to list the plants
and animals found in their
countries, to set up more
nature reserves and national
parks, and to manage forests in
a sustainable way.

Eco Thought

As many as 300 million people may
depend on the rainforests, including
farmers, healers, timber merchants,
rubber tappers and the rainforest tribes.

By keeping to forest
paths like this one,
visitors will not damage
too many forest plants.

28

In Uganda, Africa, children help to grow new trees to plant in the rainforest.

This structure, the 'Tree of Life', was made for the Earth Summit in Rio de Janeiro, Brazil, in 1992.

Rainforest charities

Some charities raise money to work with rainforest peoples. Others set up nature reserves to protect wildlife. We can help to protect the rainforests by supporting these charities.

The challenge for the future is finding ways for people to live in rainforests, find sufficient food in them, earn a living from them and look after them, all at the same time.

Taking Part

Arrange for your school to support the work of rainforest charities by selling goods such as T-shirts, recycled writing paper and candles.

Fact file

Area of rainforest

The forested areas of the world cover just over a quarter of the Earth's land area, or 3,442 million hectares. About half of these forests are found in and around the tropics.

Rich in wildlife

Rainforests are home to nine out of ten monkeys and apes, four out of ten of all birds of prey, eight out of ten of the world's insects and six out of ten of all known plants.

Deadly frog

The poison arrow frog of South American rainforests is one of the deadliest animals alive. Only one hundred-thousandth of a gram of poison from its skin can kill a human.

Giant flower

The largest flower in the world is produced by the rafflesia plant. It grows in the rainforests of South-east Asia. The flower is up to 91 centimetres across and weighs up to 11 kilograms.

Protected forest

Manu National Park at the head of the Amazon River in Peru is one of the largest rainforest national parks in the world. It covers one-and-a-half million hectares and was set up to protect wildlife and the way of life of the people of the forest. There are at least 1,000 species of bird, 13 species of monkey, 110 species of bat and 15,000 species of plant there – and there are still many more waiting to be discovered.

Loss of forest

Rainforests are disappearing at a rate of about 17 million hectares a year, an area larger than Switzerland. This works out at about one football field a second.

Trees versus beefburgers

More than half the land of Central America has been cleared to create pasture for grazing cattle. In Costa Rica, beef production went up by nearly four times between 1960 and 1980. The beef was sold to foreign countries primarily to make burgers. In the same time, local people cut back on eating beef by about half. The average Costa Rican eats less beef in a year than the average domestic cat in the United States.

A major shortfall

About six times as much tropical rainforest is cut down each year than is replanted.

Some good news

In 1997, over 20,000 hectares of rainforest were replanted in Central America.

GLOSSARY

Aquatic Living in water.

Atmosphere The layer of air that surrounds the Earth. Air is a mixture of gases.

Cash crops Crops that are grown to sell (often overseas) as a main source of money.

Condense A change in state from a gas form to liquid, such as water vapour changing back to liquid water.

Conserve To protect habitats and wildlife.

Decomposer An organism, such as a fungus, that breaks down or rots dead material.

Drought A long period without rain. A drought may last weeks or months.

Environment Everything in the surroundings, including plants, animals, rocks, water and air.

Epiphyte A plant that grows on the trunk or branches of a tree, not doing any harm.

Equator An imaginary line around the middle of the world.

Erosion The wearing down of land by wind and water, which gradually removes the soil and rocks.

Evaporate To change in state from liquid to a gas. Rain evaporates as it is heated by the warmth of sunlight.

Extinct When all individuals of a species have died out.

Government A group of people who run a country.

Habitat The place where a plant or animal lives. Habitats include forests, rivers and seas.

Nature reserves Land set aside where wildlife is protected.

Nutrients Chemicals that are needed for the healthy growth of plants and animals.

Plantation Large pieces of land where crops or trees are grown.

Pollute To poison the air, water or land.

Renewable Something that can be replaced or regrown, for example trees, or a source of energy that never runs out, such as the Sun or wind.

Resources The raw materials that are used to make things, for example wood, oil, gold.

Species A particular type of plant or animal. Different species cannot breed together.

Sustainable Able to keep up a way of life or keep resources over a long time.

Temperate Regions of the world which have mild climates and distinct seasons.

Timber Wood used in building.

Trade Selling and buying goods.

Tropical To do with the tropics. A tropical climate is hot and often wet.

Tropics The tropical regions of the world, which stretch between the Tropic of Cancer and the Tropic of Capricorn. These are two imaginary lines north and south of the Equator.

Vapour Tiny droplets of liquid like moisture in the air.

Index